EMERGI

AN ILLUSTRATED MEMOIRE

ILLUSTRATED AND WRITTEN BY

CINDY LOUISETTE JOHNSON

Copyright ©2019 Cindy Louisette Johnson
All rights reserved.
No part of this book may be used or reproduced in any manner whatsoever
without prior permission from the publisher.

ISBN 978-0-9977749-0-0
First Edition
Printed in China

Published by
The Design Group Press, LLC

About The Author:

Cindy Louisette Johnson is a painter, mixed-media artist and writer. She lives with her husband two children and chocolate standard poodle in a woodland getaway. The forests offer sanctuary and stimulation for her creativity. Books have also played a major influential role in Cindy Louisette's life from the time she was a small girl. The richness of words, ideas, pictures, adventures and people's stories engaged her mind and broadened her horizons.

Nothing pleases Cindy more than a stroll through her gardens, cooking something wonderful for family or friends, a good book or a whimsical surprise.

Her writing and art deal with the issues of her heart as it travels through life, sharply contrasted by traumatic turmoil due to severe childhood abuse and wondrous love and beauty. She is continually challenged to make her theology her biography.

She is available for speaking engagements.
Contact information:
Email: cljdesigns1@gmail.com or cindy@cindylouisette.com
Website: cindylouisette.com

EMERGENCE

The shroud of obscurity and disguise is rent;
an era of lies and untruths spent.

My deepest soul unveiled, brought to debut;
bright shining light, oh wonder of truth.

Come forth in brilliant manifestation,
make known, receive validation.

Not as the emergence of a delicate butterfly,
but in wild exuberance, shrieking across the sky.

Like stampeding horses, screaming with zeal,
dancing with ecstasy, I will reveal:

Uncontained beauty, creativity unleashed,
escaped to "Be," from darkness released!

PROLOGUE

EMERGENCE

from DARKNESS

to LIGHT.

Sitting quietly. Pen in hand. I ask God to speak.

Waiting, open to the voice of God, the thoughts that come to my mind never cease to amaze and delight me. They are usually so diametrically opposed to my own reasoning that it's unmistakably clear as to their origin. God promised to be our counselor, guide, the light unto our path; and, indeed, he is ever present and willing to make himself known; *"if you will seek me, I will be found."* (Jeremiah 29:13)

My history ... His story.

All my growing-up years were abusive to an extreme, and life was tenuous at best. There were no certainties that allowed for the building of a structural framework for psychological and emotional wellbeing.

An integral part of this abuse was the creation of a world where everything I knew to be true was built on falsehoods and lies. Many of the caregivers and role models of childhood betrayed me – purposefully penetrating my trust, so that domination and control were more easily achieved.

But, Jesus Christ, lover of my soul, had great plans for me.

As I learned from Psalms 139, prayer was essential: *"Search me oh God, know me, and lead."* And, as promised in Jeremiah 31:3-4, all along my journey he shed light on many amazing truths and promises, building an undergirding for my life of strength, verity, and unconditional love: *"I have loved you with an everlasting love; I have drawn you with loving-kindness. I will build you up again and you will be rebuilt."*

God began whispering to me of my beauty and uniqueness, often rendezvousing with me over magnificent feasts of his creation; re-parenting me with his love.

As my warrior, he had already subdued and conquered my enemies and would regain the territories of my geography that I had unknowingly lost to the Evil One.

As my lover and muse, he delivered lavish gifts of nature, daily loading me with his blessings, inspiring a "fling yourself over the edge" attitude of total trust in his magnificent power. And with these wondrous gifts, he gave me the eyes with which to see them and be utterly thrilled.

Extreme night terrors and horrifying memories savagely threatened my psychological wellbeing, but the arms of my comforter were all-encompassing, stroking my soul, and singing his love into me.

My heart at last at peace, the spirit dressed me in splendid frocks of radiant beauty, and stunning light, creating a most desired bride for her groom.

God, my Father, teaches me what a father is, offering unconditional, no-strings-attached love. Instructing, correcting, but ever-so-playfully simply showing me how to be.

Imagine that! Oh joy! His immanent goodness is an unfailing truth on which I can securely stand. He will never hurt or betray me. He is the ferocious protector of my soul – for I am his child, divinely created in his image; he gave up his son for me!

Embracing my re-purposed life.

So it was by grace, not abandonment, that I was brought to realize that the horrific atrocities of my life were an amazing preordained gift of love.

Writer Jean Guyon's thoughts helped me make sense of things, illuminating for me an understanding that whatever the adversary intended to usher into my life to utterly destroy me had to be cleared through God first; and, by the time it hit my life, it was re-purposed for my good!

Oswald Chambers further supported this idea in his work, *"My Utmost For His Highest."* He taught me that God will not allow our destruction by the enemy. He reserves that right for himself; gently crushing us into broken bread and poured out wine to minister to others.

So I will praise you, dear God. Through the enemy's plans for my demise, you have thrown me into a vigorous pursuit of you – resulting in an awakening and a return to who you created me to be.

The writings and art of my journey to being.

It seemed important to make a visual statement in this book – along with the words of my journals – to portray the deepest most intrinsic message from my soul possible.

I have come to realize that pain and suffering are universal; some people experience less, some more. Distilled to their essence, this pain and suffering can become your most precious gifts. As Tim Hansel so aptly said in his book, *"You Gotta Keep Dancing"*: *"You'll never know the height of joy til you know the depth of sorrow."*

Don't be afraid of the pain or sorrow in your life. Embrace it and allow it to be your teacher, healer, and ultimate invitation or path to continual intimate encounters with God.

It is my hope that readers of this book are encouraged by my emergence from darkness to light to seek to uncover their own personal treasures of darkness – to experience their own emergence.

With warmest regards,

Cindy Louisette Johnson

THE STAGES of MY
EMERGENCE
~~~~~~~~~~

CHRYSALIS

THE BLINDNESS of BEFORE
8 - 25

metamorphosis

THE STRUGGLE of BECOMING
26 - 61

Release

THE LIGHT of AWAKENING
62 - 89

FREEDOM

THE JOY of LETTING GO
90 - 113

CHRYSALIS

THE

BLINDNESS

OF

BEFORE

COLOR BETWEEN THE LINES

Deliberate infliction of excruciating anguish and pain
To break a child's will, compliance to gain.
Robbing the innocent of their integrity.
Purposefully undercutting any morality.

Forcibly shoving child's true self into darkness of subconscious void.
Parasitically bullying the host, intentional domination employed.
Puppeteering the young one, their purpose to serve.
Denying his essence, destroying his verve.

Chained in the prison of mediocrity,
Sobbing for my soul's lost identity.
Someone screaming, "**YOU MUST COLOR BETWEEN THE LINES**."
Unflinching, harsh, boundaries my heart defines.

"Obey the rules, no exceptions please..."
Or my life and all I love they'll most surely seize.
Dictatorial, everything black and white,
Black and white, black and white, day and night.

Cut and dry, no in between, strictly by the edict.
Oppressive deception, unyielding demands, press me to submit.
No shades, no tints, no tones or variations.
My soul constrained in a one-dimensional prison.

Someone screams, "**YOU MUST COLOR BETWEEN THE LINES**."
"Exact precise, black and white; no room for error," the voice whines.
Perfection demanded, mistakes punished, driven to perform.
But, somewhere in my deepest heart, the Immanent Presence does transform.

To Black and white, He brings Light, Truth to shatter capture.
Subverting chaotic pandemonium to harmonious rapture.
Come to my dungeoned heart, my shackles to release,
Redeeming authentic self, integrating total peace.

Presence of the Light reflects, all rays of color
Victoriously flashing through the dark, creating a beautifying stupor.
All Hell's demons scream in rage, laid prostrate by His glory,
Blinded by God's only Son, of which we're each His-Story.

Glory, Glory, Glory

I SCRIBBLE COLOR EVERYWHERE.

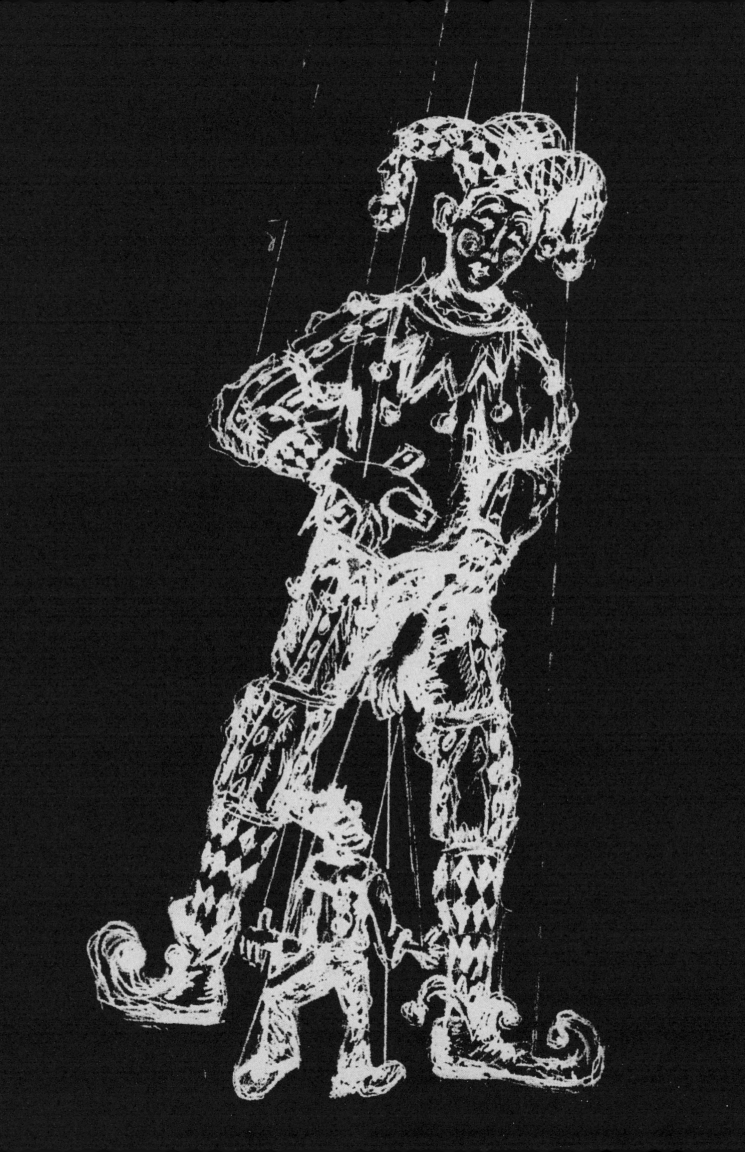

Learning to Color Outside the Lines.

In the midst of betrayal, God planted hope.

Looking back at the horrific abuse that infused my childhood, it seems ironic that my deeply wounded, misguided father was involved in children's ministries, preaching a "fire and brimstone" message, completely void of God's love and mercy.

Thankfully, the presence of God's goodness pursued my heart at a very young age, which made it clear that it was the authentic living word that was encamped in my tiny soul – nourishing and keeping my spirit strong in the midst of this sadistic dichotomy.

Although there were multigenerational strongholds in my family, God's love and mercy embedded a seed of hope deep within me. In spite of the chaos in parts of my life, as my true friend, God delightfully bestowed many treasures upon me: astounding sunsets, beautiful feathers, soaring birds, flowers and trees, wind-songs and sky-songs, crystals, forests and roaring ocean waves, butterflies, grasshoppers, toads, clouds, icicles, rendezvous in the woods for secret trysts with him, and books – precious books.

Often, he would even sing lullabies to my soul!

Searching for my authentic self.

The severity of the maltreatment I received as a child caused me, from an early age, to create protective facades and subconsciously bury my "true self" deep in the recesses of hinterland obscurity, nowhere to be found.

Addictions that society applauds — such as overachieving, work-a-holism, perfectionism, and people-pleasing — ambushed me unaware to compensate for the pain entombed deep within me.

Robbed of my "authentic self," I searched for her everywhere; in scholastic achievement, athletic performance, business and career accomplishment, creating beauty in gardens, interior design and gourmet cooking. But, to no avail. I always returned to a void.

My end became my beginning.

I would run and run, this way and that, busy-busy-busy, working-working-working, "super performing," until, some days, I would crash and burn.

During that short interval of halting, a blueness or aching sadness would envelope me.

Surprised, I would think, "What is this about?" Because, to the world at large, happiness was my mantra. But inside, I sensed something was wrong.

Repeatedly, I asked God to reveal the truth. Yet no answer seemed to be forthcoming. And, so, the dysfunctional pattern played itself over and over like a broken record. I voraciously read — searching, foraging — for what, I did not know, but something, anything.

AND SO BEGAN MY TRUTH QUEST.

The process (and indeed it's been a progressive evolution), has been slow and arduous, revealing tidbits at a time, probably all that I could tolerate at each moment, considering the grimness of my existence.

Operating in the dark, not knowing what to look for, drudging up lost, buried, archives, I asked my God-friend to be my lamp, guiding my path. And he answered to me: "Trust me, you don't need a light, just trust me! Listen for my voice and you'll know where I AM."

Thus, he hurried ahead of me, down the spiraling corridor of my interior, leaving me frozen in fear and darkness. The echoes of his voice faded away to nothingness. I rushed to catch up so as not to be left alone in the dark, cringing, mincing, stumbling all the way. There were great chasms to forge, dangerous slippery slopes to climb, and a bottomless abyss close to the infernal regions of Hell over which I had to find passage. All the while, God the spirit, God my friend, reassuringly called out to me: "Here I AM, follow me. I know the way."

THE BATTLE FOUGHT IN THE MIDDLE OF AN ORDINARY LIFE.

Meanwhile, how does one navigate unknown oceans of fear and terror and still project somewhat of a sense of normalcy in family and the world? Because this has not been a quick weekend jaunt into the darkness and back — but a laborious cross-country journey, straight through Hell, on foot, with deficient equipment.

"All out war," my enemy proclaims. "She's mine, let her go; she's my Persephone" (the Grecian mythological girl who was abducted and forced to become Queen of Hades).

Not to be subdued, my ally replies, "The battle's on. Goodness will desecrate and destroy Evil."

Dragged into battle, aided by God my warrior, we fight side-by-side for my soul. Most often, my warrior carries me in to the plunder and siege of my captured territories. Defeat is preeminent without his help. I humbly bow in gratitude.

I AM
    the Light and the Truth,
    overcoming all,
    charging through eternity,
    to set captives free!

As my sword, he hacks our way through Hades, pioneering a path, and plants my feet on solid ground singing his victorious song into my being: "I will lay my soul upon you, whispering my music across the strings of your heart. Songs of love and beauty. I AM your savior. To you I impart total healing.

Joy and jubilation pervade my mortal being, resounding praise to God and King who's brought me liberty! May all the earth proclaim this praise, for each has history. He's come to conquer sin and death and set the prisoners free!

    And with my freedom ...
    I will color outside the lines.

Illuminator

Plastic wrapped, bound in layers of helplessness;
Hampered, hindered, fastened by fear and distortion;
Captured unawares, cocooned in mummified skins of
self deceit;
Daily schlepping along, bumping against
definitive confines.

Ricocheted inward, spiraling deep in light quest;
Arduously foraging dense underbrush of beguilement;
Attacked, misled by counterfeit elixirs;
Cunning soul buccaneer rages: "All out war."

Catapulting enticing antidotes, restorative placebos,
promising panaceas and cure-alls.
Alluding alluring therapeutic relief.
Halt!
Only a bewitching mirage!
Decoy!

Encamped in the trenches of my essence,
Warrior leads,
running undercover reconnaissance.
Machete of Truth in hand;
hacking, clearing footholds into enemy territory;
Launching missiles of Light,
revealing suffocating protective membranes of
false facades;
Illuminating actuality, gently stripping away
artificial veneer.

War-torn, tattered, thick in the throes of battle,
My self-made identity agonizes to let go in death.
Screaming pain of new birth entry,
Alas, victory is won!

SUCCOR

My soul does cry for succor, Lord.

Lay me on your breast.

My heart and mind do You implore:

Nourish me with your rest.

Gently stroke my thirsting heart.

Enfold my in Your arms.

Lullaby me with Your love.

Quiet me, bring me calm.

Finding My Treasure of Calm

When arriving in my beloved Santa Barbara for a small respite, I always stay at a quaint Mediterranean lodge across the road from the ocean. From there it is convenient to walk to restaurants, beach, harbor, or "tram it" to world-class shopping.

On this particular trip, half of my baggage weight was taken up by books begging to be read, drawing tablets to be illustrated, journals to expound in … I'm always overly ambitious about what might be accomplished. It was to be a little breather from everyday demands clamoring for my attention, and was a welcome gift.

Blessed with two late-life children only twelve months and four days apart in age, a husband, a puppy, gardens to attend, a home to create and breathe a soul into; life moves at a fast clip.

I was also still in the habit of imbibing — rather indiscreetly — in one of the many vices I had learned to employ to compensate for a very traumatic growing-up experience. I would become alarmed by my over indulgence to the point of vomiting — spewing self-chastisement and caustic criticism all over myself. I felt trapped in this vicious, helpless cycle, revolving around the escape, then degradation, then shame. It seemed the conniving enemy was continuing to have victory long after leaving the home (or, I should say, "house") of my parents. I was, once again, devastated.

Into the night, my savior came.

While crying myself to sleep, I was awakened this first Santa Barbara night by the overwhelming sense of my spiritual lover's presence. Held in his tender embrace, I was caressed with words of adornment: "You are lovely, my precious one; you're the desire of my heart, my bride; allow me to hold you and stroke your soul."

His endearing affection was all that I needed for my wounded spirit to be elevated to a position of desirability and honor. The joy of our loving tryst overrode the negative demeanor of my inadequacies. I was dressed in stunning garments of grace and beauty. So sweet was the spiritual presence that permeated the moment, I longed to linger indefinitely in this haven. And sleep finally came.

Morning brought a renewed onslaught of repudiating, self destructive thoughts, wrapped in a vague remembrance of the midnight rendezvous; and the distress of this flawed state was brought to mind by my aching gut and overall sick feeling.

Armed with a cup of coffee, meandering in misery, it occurred to me to invite him to accompany me for the day. I would follow his lead, instead of lying in the gutter of self-depreciation.

TOGETHER, WE WALKED THE BEACH.

HIS PRESENCE WAS EVERYWHERE: IN THE LANDSCAPE AND OCEAN COASTLINE, IN THE ENORMOUS EUCALYPTUS TREES, WITH THE DOLPHINS SURFING OFF SHORE, EVEN IN THE PUNGENT SALT AROMA SATURATING THE SOUTHERN CALIFORNIA AIR.

BY MIDDAY HE DIRECTED ME TO BEAUTIFUL BUTTERFLY BEACH; WHO COULD HELP BUT DRINK IN THE SEA AIR SOAKED IN SUNSHINE WITH ROARING-WAVE SURROUND-SOUND? ALL OTHER SOUNDS WERE SIMPLY ELIMINATED. I WAS, AT LAST, RELEASED INTO ABSOLUTE CALM.

DIALED DOWN TO SUBLIMINAL AWARENESS, THE BEACH WALK BEGAN. I'VE WALKED MANY BEACHES IN MY LIFE — EAST COAST AND WEST COAST, MEXICO, CARIBBEAN, ITALY, FLORIDA, CAROLINAS, ARABIA, MONTE CARLO, TRINIDAD. AND I'M ALWAYS MESMERIZED BY THE RHYTHM OF THE WAVES, THE FREEDOM OF THE AIR, AND THE HOPE OF FINDING TREASURES. IN GENERAL, IT'S JUST A MAJOR RELEASE FOR ME!

WALKING ALONG THIS PARTICULAR DAY, HIS PRESENCE, HIS THOUGHTS, AND THE SIGHT AND SOUND OF THE WAVES STEADILY ROLLING IN AND OUT, CAUSED ME TO CONTEMPLATE HIS GREATNESS. HE IS INFINITELY MORE POWERFUL THAN THE SEA POUNDING TO THE SHORE — BUT THE METAPHORICAL VISUAL OF HIS CHARACTER HAVING THE STRENGTH OF AN OCEAN TO WASH OVER AND OVER ME, SMOOTHING OUT THE RAGGED EDGES OF MY LANDSCAPE HAD A PROFOUND IMPACT.

The waves of his soul smoothed me gently.

Often I ask him to take me deeper into his love, aware that this would be healing, the ultimate fulfilling, but I am usually so busy blindly thrashing about sputtering to stay in control that his presence is unnoticed.

Thankfully, his spirit thwarted my attempt to govern this day, simulating the sensation of literally being plunged to the bottom of the ocean.

As his mighty arm dragged me down into the briny depths, my flailing, churning mind desperately fought for air — for survival. Breathless, dying, disarmament was required. I prayed: "Empty me so that I might live; plunge me to the depths of your love; thrashing, churning, ever yearning, disarm me. Once emptied, pour the living water of your being into mine."

The elimination of all the extraneous yearning and subconscious flapping about in search of happiness and fulfillment ironically simplified my life. Self out of the way enabled him to fill me with the infinite vastness of himself, consequently greatly multiplying me — always the opposite of logic.

Most often, when walking a beach, after taking in the beauty of the water's magnificence, my head is bent downward searching the sand for treasures. It occurred to me (with a little divine prompting, I might add), that today's prize was "calm." I could sit for hours mesmerized by the rhythmic meter of roaring waves, tranquilizing me, bringing a stillness to my soul. My prayer poured out…

My beach prayer.

"I am treasured with your calm. I am overwhelmed by your grace. The morning began in such a state of mental wreck, and I gratefully receive your loving acceptance. I am overwhelmed, as if covered or buried beneath a mass of something, as flood waters; submerged; deluged."

I shook my head in amazement. God brought about the realization that the enemy could overwhelm me — crush drown or conquer me — with destructive lies about inadequacies, turning self-criticisms inward, masochistically eating me alive; but he, the lover of my soul, springboarded from my failures to dazzle me with his startling love and favor.

Amazing love, how can it be? That thou my God would die for me. (As stated in Charles Wesley's song, "And Can It Be").

In writing this journal entry about "calm," I cringed at seeing my nemesis (something that a person cannot conquer, the opponent or rival whom a person cannot best or overcome; undoing; affliction, kiss of death) in writing — taking ownership for it — no longer a secret, but a reality. If everyone knows, will they all hate me, think I'm weak, or less than?

So very human, not Christian, but damned human!

I sometimes wonder at my thoughts that I need to be punished or pay requital according to merits for what I was forced to be involved in as a child and the facades that consequently developed for survival.

God loves me in my very humanness — my fragilities — in my secretive garbage dumps. He's not afraid I'll infect him; he never puts on rubber gloves and a mask but purely loves me in my stench and disease and suffering. It's from here that I realize, in a broken way, how very much I need him and he does not run from me, sickened by my foul odor, but holds me ever closer in unconditional love.

My God, my God, I cannot comprehend your love but I am so in need of it. I surrender myself into your arms — your healing touch. My desire is to honor you, but in my weakness, I feel that I desecrate you, that I am useless, defeated, "unballastable," expendable, trivial, and nonessential, only darkening the way; and, stumbling, creating a muddled obstruction. And yet, in this deeply fallen state, you shine through me. You are my strength, my power, my sustenance, not me. I can only exist because of you. You are so gracious; thank you for your mercy, your hope, your reason unto me to live and be!

Sabotage, spiraling into self-destruction, met with endearing encounter, uplifting soul, wooed by my spiritual lover, brought calm that day, a great treasure of peace. And it became a portal into eternal love and acceptance, which I may revisit at any time.

TREASURE

May the waves of Your Soul smooth me gently,
Plunge
    Me
        Into
            The
                Depths
                    Of
                        Your
                            Love.

Thrashing, churning, ever yearning,
Disarm me;
    Pour
        Your
            Being
                Into
                    Mine.

Simplify, multiply.
Treasure me with your calm.

Stay, Stay, Stay Awhile

In quiet contemplation, You always draw near.
Encamped in my soul, oh Savior, You are so dear.
Your sweet presence charms my heart.
Your very aroma doth healing impart.

Stay, stay, stay awhile longer.
Satisfy my ever-growing hunger.
Sing to me for my pleasure.
The joy You bring cannot be measured.

Peace, precious peace, floods through my being,
Calming and quieting any clamor that is stewing.
You sing: "Hush, hush now, my beloved child."
Enveloping me with Your love, my enemies You beguile.

Stay, stay, stay, I pray.
Linger on throughout the day.
That I forever in You might abide,
Under Your wing my, heart and soul do hide.

metamorphosis

The
Struggle
of
Becoming

paper dolls: a self portrait

We had a great summer. It seemed to go so quickly – between a family trip to Litchfield by the Sea, ten days in our beloved Santa Barbara with Grandpa, sailing every week with an overnight on the boat, swimming often at the pool, and tons of sleepovers for our eleven- and twelve-year-old daughter and son.

With kids home from school, an overly active, fast-growing standard poodle pup, gardens to maintain, and family gyrations in general, I hadn't even cracked the door of my studio once; no writing, no mixed-media creations, no painting – nada, nothing, zip. All excuses aside, a creative mental block was probably also impeding my productivity. Prior to summer, virtually nothing had gone on in the imaginative department either, starting as far back as the previous winter holidays.

I was hoping to get into some kind of routine that included rejuvenating my parched artistic spirit, exploring different mediums to see where they might lead. That was easier said than done. Barely into a rhythm of the first week at school, we had left town for four days to attend a wedding in Detroit. We came back home to sick kids, followed by house guests for five days. Just when it seemed like reprieve was in sight, a riddling memory of abuse from my childhood blindsided me with a devastating gut punch of darkness.

I finally dragged my tattered spirit up to my studio and stared with numbness at all the wonderful supplies and bins of treasures waiting to be given life. Yet my soul was depleted. Any artful direction or ideas were far removed and inaccessible.

Sitting there, looking around for inspiration, I opened a book on paper dolls that was lying on the floor. Paper dolls had been a source of intrigue to me for quite some time. Thumbing through the illustrations once again aroused the desire to make a paper doll, maybe of myself.

Where to begin?

aNgEL giRl

I considered using the body of a fashion model as the base where I would begin, with other details added to make a mixed-media statement. Flipping through magazines, a picture of a model in ragged jeans, fitted leather jacket, and high heels caught my attention. I would wear that; it would say something about me.

A match box with a great "old world" depiction of an angel laid on my art table. The portrayal pleased me very much. Angels, not just any angels, but "old world" images, carry a special spot in my heart. I look for unique renderings every year for Christmas cards and keep a file of any stimulating interpretations. In memories of severe childhood trauma, I often have a sense of angelic presence that was dispatched to help me and do warfare on my behalf.

The matchbox representation was ideal for the doll's head. Its hands were clasped or folded at her heart in prayer. How perfect was that! The addition of an eye communicated the message that the vision of her heart was always in communion. This seemed to emphasize a comforting truth brought to my attention in Jean Guyon's writings discovered on the journey of overcoming early childhood and adolescent maladies. It proclaimed, *"If you seek God, He will be found."* The significance of this axiom has been enlightening for me, continually propelling me to ask God to take me deeper into his love, which ultimately brings healing.

Angel Girl also has a bird cage, with a lock and key dangling from her belt – representing her soul's imprisonment, but indicating that release, with the proper key, is within her grasp. She has a jewel on her forehead and belt, signifying she is treasured by God.

Affixed to Angel Girl's side is a gorgeous Borzois dog – named Deidre. This was a dog I loved very much as a child. She was used to coerce me into doing my captors' bidding at the time. But, despite this malevolent intent, Deidre and I bonded at the hip and heart, and my spirit was fed by her loyalty and love for me – once again, foiling the plans of the Dragon.

{more...}

CagE giRl

Not wanting to take my eyes off of Angel Girl, yet mentally wishing to do another paper doll, I leafed through other materials that had touched me or caught my attention.

A representation from *Cloth, Paper, Scissors Magazine* (Sept/Oct. 2012 ed.), featuring a Santos art doll, captured my heart. Attaching the upper body of this beauty to a model's lower body I thought, "Yes, this is Cage Girl." She represents my heart and soul that were held hostage from early childhood.

This comprehension has taken a lifetime to uncover and allow God the illuminator to identify and break the shackles, releasing me from their bondage. She has a beautiful spirit in spite of her imprisonment, carrying flowers and stars and a banner of PEACE

Her God has always been with her, even through the harrowing experience of being "caged" all of her growing-up years, not knowing how to get out.

mAsQuERaDE giRl

The next doll to come into existence was Masquerade Girl. In the back of my mind there were remembrances of events and occasions where everyone was masked and "dolled" up in costume, incognito of their true identities. This camouflage allowed them to reveal their raw or naked selves, enabling them to come forth without accountability or shame, to perform illicit deeds with no liability.

Beautiful "Masquerade Girl" was likewise disguised; very sought-after, often betrayed, but proverbially blessed as the Queen of Hearts. Almighty God purveyed her with a queen heart to survive, and sustenance to prevail. He sent her birds and feathers and a sundry of pleasures to help her survive the incriminations against her. Her spirit could not be robbed of its beauty.

NATuRE giRl

Nature Girl was then brought into being – appareled
   in a long, cozy, grey sweatshirt dress, jacketed with a black
leather sleeveless vest, finished out in black, slouchy boots. She
         sports a pair of butterfly wings and is headed up by a
      crowned nuthatch.

A honey bee and heart, in the vicinity of her bodice, remind her to
         "bee" true to herself, which is exceedingly difficult in light
   of the many facades she has developed to protect her severely
mistreated soul.

         Her butterfly wings signify her process of
metamorphosis as she navigates the excavation of hidden truths buried
   deep within her.

The bird head and wings also bring her pleasure, appealing to her
   lively imagination. God the creator often sends them to his girl
         as a reminder that he is ever present amidst the calamities
   she faces – his very presence overriding and foiling Evil's intent.
Her friend the toad, another delightful companion from nature,
         represents the fact that things are not always what they
      appear to be. Toad is Nature Girl's prince, bridegroom, and lover
         of her soul, overseeing her transformation from
darkness to the light.

         Throughout Nature Girl's life, rendezvous in the woods connect
         her on a deep level with her God the lover,
emancipator, and deliverer.

NATuRE giRl

{more...}

UnMaskiNg tHe TRuTH

Looking over the first four paper dolls, I found it interesting that they were all donned with a disguise. Surprised, upon returning to the "masks" of my past, it occurred to me that they weren't concealments, but really who I am – segmented, compartmentalized, buried, but WOW! truly who I am.

That was enlightening! No wonder the current facades I sported, carrying a semblance of truth, left me empty, bored, and continually searching for more.

The following quote in Madeleine L'Engle's "The Irrational Season," so aptly pertained to this masquerade:

> *"We are taught early, very early, to set up false expectations of ourselves, and when we fall away from pearly-pink perfection we have supposed to be our 'real self,' and are faced with what is in fact our real self, we alibi and rationalize and do everything we can to avoid seeing it. And far too often we succeed, and then we are like my psychiatrist friend's patients who are afraid to remember, because if their memories are true, then their present lives are false."*

A Life in Collage

I sensed that there were other paper dolls that
needed to be designed – like Cello Girl, Equestrian Girl,
and Fashion Girl – but, for the moment, my heart
led me in a different direction.

Mentally not ready to complete any more paper dolls, my
mind needed to explore a self-portrait in collage form.
Browsing through magazines and pictures already on file, I
began a five-hour task of cutting, pasting, and piecing together the
story of my life – totally absorbed, unable to stop until it was finished.

The impact of seeing what I knew to be true at a cognitive level was
almost shocking to me in a visual or pictorial dimension. It
had a profound effect in the emotional realm, carrying a much more
poignant message than words ever could.

Standing back in amazement, observing that the essence of
my life – all its pain, subversive control, soul imprisonment, hope,
and heavenly aid – was able to be captured with a few torn out
pictures, it dawned on me that divine intervention in this process was
most certainly present. The schematic I had created rendered a
gut wrenching "great sadness" that had always been
lurking in the background of my life, but it also depicted a blessed
hope and ever-present help and comfort.

Broken But not destroyed

Along the pathway of this journey many well-meaning people have said to me: just claim Psalms 91 and no further harm will come to your life.

Contemplating that passage, together with the facts of my life, I realized they derived that conclusion out of the fear of not wanting bad things to happen to good people. But, in light of Biblical history, we know that John the Baptist was beheaded, Peter was hung, and Jesus Christ himself was crucified!

The passage does, however, promise that God will not allow our spirit to be broken into destruction, and he has kept that pledge to me. Oswald Chambers portrayed the idea that God will not allow the enemy to completely destroy you; he reserves that right for himself. He will crush you (gently, tenderly, I might add) and make you poured-out wine and broken bread for the feeding of the Body.

A Spirit-Led Journey

It is quite apparent to me that this unveiling process has long been underway; it was no coincidence that I was able to find the right pictures.

Last year there seemed to be an unspoken mission to go through children's books and pull images that caught my eye. When I came across a model with pearled headgear it reminded me of my "soul incarceration," communicating the horrific sadness I felt deep within me. And yet, in spite of that angst, there was also a kind of joy. Amazing how the two can coexist.

My maker always delighted me with birds and feathers, treasures he would bring me from nature. The pictures I found that allowed me to create an image of small hands sending up a butterfly kite from inside my jailed heart represent my intact spirit calling for help from the heavens. And, in response to when my spirit was tattered, my helper would send me angels.

Through this process, I have learned that his very presence trumps any evil, overriding it with beauty. The consciousness came to me that, as a child, he camped out in my heart; literally – pitched his tent and lullabied my spirit – sweet Jesus, lover of my soul.

Shooz

Familial dissonance dictates childhood confusion.
Baffled, perplexed with tumultuous commotion.

Natural recourse assuages, diverts, relieves,
Formulating false systems of beliefs.

Food, drink, performance, or extraneous pleasures
Clamor to appease in most comforting measures.

Retreating, denying our true authenticity.
False facades smother us with a voracity.

Our "lost" self cries in pain,
As if wearing the wrong sized shoe in vain.

Demanding, we walk in uncomfortable stilettos,
Soldiering our way through the world with a "fierce machismo."

Certainly cannot run, skip, hop, or jump for joy.
Creativity blistered, robbed, deceived in this ploy.

Crippled, "out of commission," can barely navigate.
Lord succor my soul, my falsehoods negate.

Is it safer to wear uncomfortable shoes?
Stay chained by my neck, willing to loose?

Than exert the brawn of genuine identity?
Veritable, bona fide, actuality?

Profound discovery, terrifying realization.
Do I choose to "numb out" or march forward eyes wide open?

It's all on my shoulders, don't retreat!
EMERGE, EVOLVE, allow my voice to SPEAK!

Take the damned shoes off and put on the pair that fits!

Sanctuary of Release

    Miracle me with healing I implore.
You give me sanctuary to restore.
    How many shades of refuge do exist?
Hideaway, haven, sanctum, retreat to subsist.

    You shroud me and conceal me in motherly under-winged manner.
Enfold me in the nest of Your soul's demeanor.
Become my fantastical tree-house from which to view
    My world through Your looking glass, to make anew.

Seeing from Your perspective,
    Recalibrate my heart's objective.
Nudge me with spirit of gratitude,
    Ever cognizant of the moments' gift You allude.

    Permeate the present I beseech.
Thereby I enter You, Sanctuary of Release.

music is the key

Studying my paper dolls and self-portrait collage, it seemed to be communicating that music was somehow a key.

Much of my growing up experience was so tethered with shocking atrocities that I had deeply buried the incidents attached to such pain. And loosing music was a critical part of it.

I remember a turning point in elementary school when I adamantly stated, "You can't make me sing, you can't make me do music, I won't," and I did not! And thus, my music was buried, entombed in a locked, sealed, sepulcher, so abysmally submerged that even I couldn't find it.

Suddenly, the phrase "music is the key" was constantly running through my mind. At the time, I happened to be reading Helene Lerner's book, "In Her Power, Reclaiming Your Authentic Self."

Often, I'll walk through a library or bookstore and invite God to show me books that will aid in piecing together the puzzle of my life. It's astounding what he brings to my attention. This was a perfect case in point.

In this book, Lerner describes a renewal weekend she attended involving an overcoming exercise where one jumped from a high platform releasing fears and demanding great trust. She was frightened to the point of being paralyzed, but finally jumped. She said she started uncontrollably sobbing, realizing she was horrified by the thought of not being in control.

When I came to this point, I paused, and thought to myself, "What scares me to death?" Gasping, as a guttural weeping lurched from the fathomless, innermost part of myself, the answer came forth – *"The music, I'm terrified of the music!"*

LoST GiFtS

In flashbacks I vaguely recalled playing the cello in my childhood, but it was as if this had occurred on another planet in another lifetime. The memory was, however, confirmed by my sister.

Similarly, all the other "gifts" – like painting, fashion design, and fluency in languages – were totally elusive to me, as if I had come out of a coma. I knew these abilities existed, but couldn't quite recollect how to perform them. There was absolutely no access. It may be how a stroke victim feels.

she was just a little girl climbing trees, searching for agates, picking wild black-eyed Susans

Initially, there was great frustration and a struggle to regain lost territory. Eventually, I settled into an attitude of: "It is what it is. I won't continue to mourn for what is lost, I'll try to move forward with what I have, and make it the best I can."

darkness descended on her

Even though my heart longed for that part of me that was taken, I knew the time or energy to relearn it all wasn't available. Bits and pieces would eek out here and there in decorating, gardening, culinary skills, and fashion design – bringing appreciated accolades, but also reminding me of all that I had lost.

her water broke she didn't know what was happening she tried to keep her alive in a shoe box under her bed her girl-child soul screaming What to do? What to do? What to do?

she decided Never to let music harm her again unknowingly disconnecting herself from her own soul

her favorite color was blue

LiSTeniNG WiTH MY heART

Reading the works of Madeleine L'Engle, I was deeply affected by her thinking on the subject of ideas and inspiration. She said, *"I am convinced that each work of art, be it a great work of genius or something very small, has its own life, and it will come to the artist, the composer, or the writer or the painter and say, 'Here I am; compose me; or write me; or paint me.' And the job of the artist is to serve the work ... All I can do, as far as activism is concerned, is to write daily, read as much as possible and keep my vocabulary alive and changing so that I will have an instrument on which to play the book if it does me the honor of coming to me and asking to be written."*

I thought, this is what I can do. I can show up and serve the ideas at hand and leave the rest to the Spirit. This seemed to take the pressure off me and negate all the adverse feedback from my internal censor who was chiding me with excuses and reasons why I shouldn't pursue my music or writing.

And yet, furthering her train of thought, L'Engle also said, *"Your head needs to have the flexibility to bend down to your heart."*

I was just beginning to listen to my heart with its inner voice when the message "music is the key" struck loud and clear. Terrified, because music was so tangled with torturous pain in my past and entombed deeply within me, I frantically thought, "I have to touch, or see, or maybe just feel a cello."

I turned to the Internet and studied musicians – how they held their hands, bowed their bows, and vibrated the strings. I saw Adam Hurst playing and thought, "Maybe I'll just do a little schematic drawing of him performing" – which turned into quite a feat, because the available image was a fleeting one.

The shadow sketch that ensued in about
    thirty seconds was amazing to me.

FiNDiNG CELLo GiRL - AND CELLo GiRL FiNDiNG ME

Several weeks before my Internet study, pen in hand,
    thinking about what other paper dolls needed to be added to
  my collection, I did a rough sketch of Cello Girl.

    This was a complete surprise to me, because drawing from
    imagination had been difficult for me and I virtually never
attempted it. I found myself sitting back and shaking my head in
    wonderment at this sketch. What was happening? If drawing was
coming more freely, what else might be released?

From another passage by L'Engle I learned that she
 often played Bach piano compositions in the evenings to stimulate her
mind and feed her soul. So, once again, on one of my library walks with
God the spirit, I asked him to select some music for
    me to listen to. He brought me to Misha Maisky playing Bach cello.

    Listening over and over again, my soul was washed with beauty,
calling "Cello Girl" out, enticing her to break away.

{more...}

BecOMing CELLo giRl

Before long, my insightful husband said, "Why not rent a cello for awhile and see what happens?" But the fear of taking such a leap was so mortifying that I could not even go to the music store by myself for fear of a meltdown. In response, my wonderful husband accompanied me.

The cello remained in the back end of the car for an entire week. I was unable to even bring it into the house.

But, doggone it, I thought, I am here and I am showing up. If the *music is the key*, then I'll trust the Lord to lead the way, even if my cello language is stroked out and aphasic.

I WILL have the courage to take baby steps.

I WILL show up and leave the rest up to God.

I MUST move forward.

It's all I know how to do; I can't shut it down – it's the **EMERGENCE** of my soul.

*Jesus how did you feel, locked in the finite, fragility
of a human body and mind? Totally frustrated?
Completely suffocated; dependent on the caregiver
in entirety? Is that the real gift ... your will ... in
your time?*

I SiNG GLORY, GLORY, GLORY to YOUR HOLY NAME

The day I bumped into Zephaniah 3:17 thrilled me to the core. It states that God as music loves us so much, he will joy over us with singing. Once, that was almost an incomprehensible thought to me – that my God would sing to me! Until I began asking him to do so ... and then, unimaginable pleasure lifted me right out of the here and now.

There are times when my heart still cries out in aching agony over the loss of my abilities. But the message that God returns to me is, "you had to die, die, die, that you might live, live, live."

Some days the adventure is exhilarating, stimulating and exciting; other days it's taxing, surgically cutting away layer upon layer of scar tissue; it is downright arduous and painful.

Often, I need God the warrior to carry me and pluck me up from where I have fallen down into cavernous, dark precipices along the way. But he is always prepared with the equipment we need – lights, ropes, pitons, first aid supplies and snake bite kits for extracting the poison of lies and deceptions.

Without him I would most surely be a permanent captor of Hades and spend an eternity of devastating mourning. And, most grievous of all – with no music!

Cello

Lay Your soul upon me.
Whisper Your music across the strings of my heart;
Songs of Your love and beauty,
Oh my Lord and Savior Thou art.

Sweet melody

In the quiet of my mind,
The Lord sings to me so sublime.
The music of His voice intoxicates my ear.
One supposes such beauty only angels hear.

His thoughts take me to another world.
Calmness, joy, around my mind, they swirl.
Revelations of His splendor enthrall me,
His tender loving kindness I see.

Oh joy, oh ecstasy, I scarce can contain;
In Your presence, I long to remain.
The world around me fades away.
Dear Jesus with You I wish to stay.

Composition

Regard my spirit, oh Symphony.
Twill round my clock in euphony.
Heaven's chorus bring to earthly mind,
Harnessing harmonic beauty in windly chimes.

Rhythmically healing, melodiously bowing,
My heart strings recalibrate, vibrating, sowing.
Color me with the tone of Your soul,
Singing me beauty, chanting all is well.

Symphonically orchestrate in pleasing medley,
Composing, underpinning, numerous my complexities;
Creating melody Your ear for to hear;
My soul substance dances bringing You near.

Poetically intertwining with Holy Triad.
Performing arias of richest myriad.
Endless are the musical scores,
When combined with eternal, infinitesimal chords.

Fulfilling within Your intended design,
My innermost parts to You do resign.
Conduct many scores in this humble architecture.
My heart sings to You in adoring genuflector.
Amen

miraculous composition

May You, as "Music," compose my melody
With intricate shades of harmonic complexity;
Vibrate my soul strings with Your virtuoso,
Override definitive familial and cultural innuendos.

Superseding simplistic Gregorian chants
Your uncontained harmony melodiously rants.
Exuberant, joyous, wildly proclaim
That You, Jesus, my author I name.

Singing me, orchestrate, choreograph me to existence,
Filling me with the beauty of Your essence.
Creating, fashioning, a unique composition
For Your Heavenly designed exposition.

Portraying Your glory in wounded and frail
Rhythmically healing ... Your goodness prevails.
The Singer proclaims His authority,
Resurrecting to life His creativity.

Hallelujah, I will dance and sing
To my Creator, my God and King.
Without You I'm deaf and I am dumb;
My soul could nary a tune or music hum.

Sing praise and glory to Heaven above,
Shedding light on Your glorious love.
You, who preside over everything,
Ubiquitous all throughout history.

Amen and Amen and Amen.
Forever transcending eternity.
So be it.

2. Joy and jubilation fill my heart

   Renewing strength and love You now impart

   Guidance and direction throughout the day

   My ear in tune and hearing as You lead the way

   Refrain:

   Heal my soul completely replenish me

   Release from tension Your calming peace I see

3. Peace Your calming peace embodies me

   My heart__ at__ rest what a victory

   All my inner yearnings that ache for more

   Sufficed by Your embrace my soul with You will soar

   Refrain:

   Heal my soul completely replenish me

   Release from tension Your calming peace I see

Release

The

Light

of

Awakening

Montaged

Thrust into helpless anxiety,
Dredging up past memories of horrific atrocities;

Undone, sucker-punched, terrorized, traumatized;
Pain so severe, frantic, my soul agonized.

Asked for healing, You bring me to my knees in devastation;
There's nothing like sorrow to get one's attention.

Splintered, fractured, shattered by the strong FIST of affliction,
Veneer, stripped by intense tribulation;

Dungeoned, battled, shackled in darkness,
My soul sings to You, claiming Your immanent goodness.

I WILL trust Your gift of pain;
Rendered helpless, WILL be my gain.

Incapacitation is not weak.
Living Words of strength salve my wounds as You speak.

Nudged to examine the meaning of montage,
It's the regrouping of fragments and pieces forming collage;

Disparate elements to form a whole,
Integration of my parts complete my soul.

Illumined by Your Presence,
Singing into me Your very Essence.

A Humpty-Dumpty Montage

While practicing the cello, which hadn't been touched in days, there seemed to be an urgency to get up and write down the word "montage" in my journal. Montage, hmmm, I don't even think I know the meaning of that word; I never use it.

Later that night, God woke me at 3:30 a.m. Lying there awhile, there was an amazing sense of being "present." It was different from being wide awake – it was really being present, whatever that meant. I thanked God for giving me a deeper insight or consciousness of his love. A crazy, wild-hare idea occurred to me. "God, did you integrate or transform me while I was sleeping? I feel so complete. Is this what it feels like to be whole?"

I got up, went to the studio, opened my journal ... and, staring back at me, was the word MONTAGE.

Of course it had to be dictionaried. Amazing. That's not a word I use or even am familiar with, but there it was: Montage ... the technique of combining in a single composition pictorial elements from various sources, as parts of different photographs or fragments of printing either to give the illusion that the elements belonged together originally or to allow each to retain its separate identity as a means of adding interest or meaning to; composition, collage, conglomerate, medley, patchwork, potpourri.

Ha! Humpty Dumpty came to my mind. God you're showing your sense of humor. It was as if you are saying: "All the kings horses and all the kings men couldn't put Humpty together again ... BUT, your brokenness is not too difficult for me. I'll create an exquisite montage of all your pieces, a masterpiece, a literal work of art."

Healing Journey

In the quiet stillness of the night,
I run to Jesus in my fight.
He whispers love, kindness, joy and peace;
my soul's anxieties to release.

The healing process, slow it seems,
peels back layers of self esteem,
rendering me naked, helpless, lost;
my new identity in the cross.

Cleansing blood wash o'er me now.
Oh Lord, to thee, that I may bow.
Patiently awaiting Your timing, Your touch.
My soul now realizes You love me so much.

Hallelujah, I praise Your name.
You're my lover, my healer, one in the same.
You agonize with me in my trials.
Interceding for victory, my enemy You beguile.

Pouring over me, to mine adversaries forlorn.
From Your plenteous fruitful horn,
blessings, gifts, treasures before unknown.
In Thee, my Lord, I make my home.

Coco: A Love Story.

Since his arrival as a Christmas gift to our daughter, large, brown poodle, Coco Bear, had won all our hearts and positioned himself as an intrinsic member of the family. In particular, he had become a soul-mate to our girl, miraculously drawing her out of her shy introversion.

Rather suddenly, to the dismay of us all, he became quite ill. For ten days, he hadn't eaten or taken in any fluids. It looked like we might lose him. My daughter's fear was deeply internalized and she was not willing to address it. But she finally sobbed, "Why does God have to take our dog?" How does a mother answer that?

A feeling of utter helplessness overtook me; a complete powerlessness, the inability to do anything. Initially it appeared that I was crying for my daughter's sake; but then, all the grief and vulnerability of every atrocity in my own life – of which there were many – blindsided me.

Flashbacks of pain from pain

Helpless, horrified, magnum-shocked, appalled, intimidated, alarmed, scared to death, sickened, aghast, repelled, frozen, and stunned. Throughout my formative and adolescent years, I had been repeatedly terrorized to the point of complete emotional, physical, and psychological shutdown. I recognized this old helpless feeling – destitute but agonizingly alive!

As the listless dog lay despondent on my lap, there seemed to be a similarity with my soul, my mind thinking, "I'm like a limp rag doll at your feet, dear God; sucker-punched and feeling incapacitated by dredged-up memories of past atrocities."

Each revisited horror brought a renewed debilitating sense of destitution. Contemplating the synonyms of helplessness, waves of immobilizing yucky sludge washed their filthy stench and mire over me.

(more...)

Thanking God for the pain

I have learned through years of working through the pain of insidious acts against me as a child that God is immanently good and does everything out of love. Thus, I decided to stand on that truth and began to thank him for the gift of this seeming calamity, electing to trust him to bring goodness to me, and my family – whether Coco lived or died.

What other choice was there? To be angry and bitter and accusatory? The enemy would gloat and scream in glee if I would decide to grovel in self-pity. He could then lambaste me with defeat, further using the past to destroy me.

Gathering up every horrific event and helpless feeling and depositing them at God's feet, my heart requested that he take them from me – re-parent me, becoming my father and mother just as scripture so consolingly promises, rubbing his deep healing balm of love into their remaining jagged scars. There is no doubt in my mind that this kind of pluck did not originate in my brain but was divinely prompted. So, grabbing onto God, the wind, my whip-lashed soul held on for dear life determining to trust the opposite direction of my own reasoning.

Many times on the path of healing, my heart has cried out to God in agony, pleading, "I have nothing to bring you except pain." To which he always replies, "Give me your pain, let go of it, release it, so that you might taste and experience my goodness."

It was not a coincidence that writer Macrina Wiederkehr's poem based on the widow of Zarephath should cross my path right at this time of deciding to be thankful and trust!

(more...)

A poem by Macrina Wiederkehr

*Having eaten my last crumb
I hear a voice in the wilderness of my heart
   Bring me a little water
    the voice pleads.
I am off for the water
when again I am interrupted
   Bring me a scrap of bread
    the voice calls.
I freeze inside, barely able to believe
   the demands of God.
It is kindness to give someone a drink, yes
But to give out of an empty house is agony.*

*Someone is asking for a crust of bread
And I have only
   a few tears
   a handful of flour
   a little oil.
The sticks in my hand
   are to build a fire,
   to bake a few crumbs for myself
   before I die.*

But the call waits in my soul
    like a volcano.
I bake the bread in silence
    with my tears
    with my handful of flour
    with my little oil.
The salt from my tears is the seasoning.

The hungry one eats and is nourished.

Suddenly I am hungry no longer
My vessel of flour is undiminishing
My jar of oil never runs dry.

When you have gathered up the crumbs
    of all you have and are
And baked your bread
    in the only place left:
    the oven of your heart,
Then you will know what it means
    to be bread for the world.

There is a wealth in poverty
    that ought not to be wasted.
There is a nourishment in crumbs
    that ought to be tasted.

Finding my own name for God

In addition to asking for the healing balm of love and re-parenting, pondering what it would be like to really know or more deeply comprehend the perfect love of my Heavenly Father, it seemed necessary to request that God provide a different name by which to refer to him other than father, dad, daddy, or Abba – because all of these carry extremely negative connotations from previous experiences. And so he graciously responded in time: I am the "lover of your soul."

My soul was also desirous for God to sing calm into me, in preparation to receive the goodness he purposed from this anguish.

"The wreckage that intense trauma and tribulation leave within a child, or any human being, shatters and splinters or fractures their being." Macrina Wiederkehr, in "A Tree Full of Angels," says, "Within the wardrobe of your brain you have many vintage costumes to outfit your states of mind and camouflage your discomfort ... i.e., perfectionists, do-gooders, self righteous, preachers, unstoppable intellectualizers ..." The author calls us to excavate our own "schemes and idiosyncratic obstacles to healthy assertiveness ... saying maladaptive schemes are derived from disquieting childhood or adolescent experiences where fundamental needs were not adequately met."

Finding blessed rest in God's beauty

In the meantime, there was still no definitive conclusion to Coco's condition. Retreating to the back garden, attempting to find a little reprieve from the pain in my heart, God's beauty consoled me. The birdbath was under-planted with blue scabiosa, fuchsia petunias, hostas and variegated lamium; particularly beautiful this spring. All the purple irises were blooming, wafting a sweet grape aroma into the air.

Determined to offer gratitude, with an expectancy of the blessings this situation would bring, God then proceeded to blow me away with an exotic gift of a scarlet tanager followed by a delicate hummingbird moth – both rarities in the garden. A quiet little flit alerted me to a wren carrying food to chirping babies nested in the flower arrangement behind me. Its partner perched on the wisteria proceeded to sing the most amazing concert. I thought, "How good you are; making your presence and care known in the midst of this emotional turmoil, continuing to express your love at every turn."

(more...)

Finding strength in weakness

In reflecting on that helpless, splintered part of me who carried and compartmentalized all the agony so that survival could be maintained, the understanding came to me that this was not weakness but required a great strength. And it became a kind of a revolutionary turnaround in my thinking.

And so, I began a synonym search for "strong," finding words to be so powerful, multidimensional. I find that each synonym I explore in this manner becomes like the crosshatching in a delineation, bringing new rich depth to the silhouette of the concept or idea giving it deeper definition, a more intrinsic illustration of the thought. The similar words are kind of a "brainstorming," if you will, bringing numerous layers of complexities and twists to the meaning. And soon, I've built a voluminous "shading" of an idea with words – a painting or contouring with words and ideas!

With "strong," I found: resolute, brave, gutsy, independent, intelligent, iron-willed, sagacious, self-assertive, plucky, powerful means to resist attack, assault, or aggression, a strong fortress, a strong defense, able to resist strain, force, and wear, of a strong cloth, decisively unyielding, firm, uncompromising.

It occurred to me as I read and reread these analogues of strength that they were actually living words of truth, acting as a cleansing antibiotic and healing ointment – taking almost immediate effect.

I thought, "I am well-made, well-founded, not weak; my being does embody all these multifaceted definitions of strength because you, God, are all those things to the infinity and I am made in your image."

Sensing that this revelation was not a false machismo but newly donned attire cut from the "strong cloth" of the House of Almighty God, I was wowed! God, the living word, miraculously applied the healing salve of strength's metonyms, literally speaking their curative power into my jagged scars, simultaneously making me very aware of what was happening. And I asked that he would do the same for Coco.

(more...)

Singing through the pain

It seemed critical to note the time of this request. In bidding him to take me deeper into his love and intense joy, which would consequently throw off the horrific sadness that always lurks in my shadows, I was not expecting to delve into treacherously gouging pain. Choosing to claim his immanent goodness, to trust in him, determined to sing his praises, he honored me with a new wardrobe – turning my frock of mourning into one of rejoicing, singing his very essence into me.

My heart echoed with words of gratitude, using the words for "strength" – not only for what he would do for Coco, but for using this beautiful animal to teach me.

I awoke in the middle of that night startled, in excruciating agony, almost to the point of being overwhelmed with a sense of extreme mind and heart agitation; horrific heartache.

Pictures of Coco running and playing were racing through my mind and my heart was acutely saddened at the thought of losing him. The intensity of the pain was so severe it dawned on me this was not just about a dog.

I didn't know if I could stand it. I've been through countless horrifying memories, but never anything as unbearably harrowing as this; frantic, feeling a need to run, scream, and pull my hair out. It was as if a thousand bees were stinging me.

My soul was plunged into the heart-wrenching black abyss of the awful helpless despair I felt at every appalling event that had ever occurred in my life. I didn't know what to do. It was unleashed, wild, crazy agony; all-out war.

Absolutely astounding to me, my heart then began to sing praises to God. There was some vague remembrance in the back of my mind of hearing that evil must flee in the face of laudation to God.

It was apparent that God the warrior had come to aid me in this wild battle of fury for my destruction, for the last thing on my mind was to sing. But the more I sang, the more the black veil began to rise. My thoughts went to Paul and Silas singing in prison in the middle of the night, their shackles falling off and they were freed. Wow! I was experiencing a present-day miracle! Nothing less!

(more...)

Finding the meaning of absolute love

Often, I ask the Lord to take me deeper into his love, sensing that I don't really even begin to comprehend it. My husband frequently tells the kids: "To know and not to do, is not to know." That idiom seemed to apply to me at that moment – to know and not to feel, is not to know.

Oh yes, theologically, the love of God in sending his Son to die for the world has been taught to me my whole life. But the meaning of that love was brought to me with a new depth of experiencing that night.

If I was willing to do anything to spare my daughter the anxiety she often faces, even buy her a dog which I didn't want, take care of him, hold him while he's vomiting, allow this huge 70-pound poodle to lie in my lap while he was distressed, and even pray that God would spare him, so my girl would not be devastated, then Almighty God, perfect Father, what lengths would you go to for your Son?

And yet, you sent him to the cross for me, for all of mankind. And if my pain tonight – so traumatic, so excruciatingly intense – is but one person's pain ... I envision that pain multiplied by every human being in every generation of the existence of the world, and still, the pain on the cross to which you knowingly sent your Son is absolutely unfathomable. Oh, my God, how much you must love me, love all of humanity, to sacrifice your only Son to bear the agonizing brunt of this intensely grotesque, wickedly evil pain and suffering.

Wiederkehr says: "In the midst of sorrow there's nothing to do but be there and celebrate the hurt. We celebrate the hurt through holy screams. Holy screams come from the heart ... The only thing the Father wishes for us is to be one with Him as He and His Son are one, so He, the most perfect, loving parent sent His only Son to the cross and had to witness the Holy Scream of His child, Jesus, for all mankind so that He might pay the price for our wholeness."

With Coco now near death, we opted for exploratory surgery. And, of course, at exactly the divinely prompted time that I prayed for God's healing touch to be placed on Pup, they found a large athletic sock wrapped around his intestine that would have killed him if not removed.

(more...)

God, Lover of My Soul

God – lover of my soul – your unspoken words are so clear, they're unmistakable. There is no doubt in my mind that you instigated our dog to ingest a sock, and bring him close to death, in order to ferret out my own pain, so that you could administer your miraculous healing to free me – your so imprisoned child – as well as heal the loving creature that you used as the instrument of this miracle.

Amazing love – lover of my soul – you're pursuing me! I love your finesse, the pleasures you bring to me, your ardent procurement of my being. I love being your prize! How could I resist you? You created me, you love me, you sing to me, you gift me with delightfully precious presents. I do adore you. You are my breath and my very sunshine!

Once again I awake late; pondering the word "integrate," I discover: to bring together, to incorporate (parts into a whole), to combine or complete, to unify, fuse, mingle, merge, conjoin. I apply them all as I contemplate the thought: "Lord you know all my parts; helpless, workaholic, perfectionist, artist, musician, creator. You created me to break into splinters to survive. Thank you! Now, you're putting me back together."

And I write down all the synonyms I found for "integrate," I think "that's what God wants to do with me – be one with me, conjoin with me. He is the master integrator."

I pray that he will bring me together – bring us together with him. The Trinity plus me equals four – my new number. In the past, evil had assigned me the number of six. Now it is four … four … four … four!

This is huge! I am not weak, I am a survivor, created by Almighty God, and now being put back together again – mended, transformed.

(more...)

"Then Sings My Soul"

    While marveling at your undeniable presence, orchestrating all of the events in the last few days, a line from an old hymn that had not been on my radar in years, came to mind. A book that lists hymns and the story of their origins, just happened to be lying next to my chair in the studio. I could not believe that this was a coincidence at 4:30 a.m. The fourth verse of the hymn that was in my mind caught my attention in particular:

Long my imprisoned spirit lay
    Fast bound in sin and nature's night,
Thine eye diffused a quickening ray,
    I woke, the dungeon flamed with light,
My chains fell off, my heart was free,
    I rose, went forth and followed thee.

    Lover of my soul, it was as if you planted the line of that song in my mind because you wanted to talk to me and tell me specifically that you had flamed my darkness with your light, unlocking the bondage of my woundedness. Thank you for pursuing my heart, making your presence so very known to me.

    Almighty God, you utterly dazzle me! I asked you for healing and you prompted Coco to ingest a sock that nearly killed him. My concern about the devastating fallout for my daughter flushed out all the horrific agony of bygone heinous incidents in my life, unearthing a previously unknown depth of suffering and anguish. Felled to my knees in pain, utterly helpless, I came to the realization that I can't change or transform myself – God knows I've tried. But I can choose to surrender or release my affliction to you. I can let go, enabling your regenerative salve to bring solace and restoration to my soul.

    The Lord will be your everlasting light,
        and the days of your mourning will be ended.   - Isaiah 60:2.

    Master artist, you then composed the most beautiful montage incorporating all of my pieces. Indeed, what an astounding love story of the lengths you will go to, to pursue my heart, kiss my soul and complete me!

Merci Beaucoup,
I will be Your treasure, oh Lover of my Soul;
Lay Your Soul upon me
Whisper Your Music across
*   the strings of my heart*
Songs of Your Love and Beauty
Oh my Lord and Savior Thou art

All is Well

Lord, my soul is crushed and torn asunder,
Immobilized by the desperate, aching pain,
    my mind does wonder.
Why did You bring me to face this atrocious calamity?
Yet, thankful is my heart for Your grace to me.

Even though I stray and wander, always You meet me
    in my deepest heart.
So tender, so caring is the love, You do impart.
Sweet Jesus, help me to grieve; my heart I know You'll heal.
This very pain, unimaginable, it's blessings You will reveal.

That I, undeserving, should receive Your bountiful grace
In my suffering distress; You disclose Your beautiful face,
Your thoughts cascade upon my soul; "it's alright, all is well,
I am Your comfort amidst this tempestuous squall."

I am Your rock, anchor Your heart in Me.
Your fortitude and strength, will I always be.
You, dear girl, are My special beloved one.
Come, let us dance before the evening sun.

May My beauty and splendor override your sorrow,
Exuding an intoxicating aroma for your tomorrows.
Come, Come and be with Me,
My lover, my bride, for eternity.

Release

My dark soul veil has been lifted;
  Your Light glimmers through the morning fog;
I sense Your presence all around me,
  Even the cool, gray mist envelopes me with warmth and
     Pleasure.
My heart sings in gratitude.
  You are always with me;
Your endless love steadies me,
  Directs my path with anticipation and hope.
Journey all the day long by my side,
  Make me ever aware of Your continual presence.

FREEDOM

The
Joy
of
Letting
Go

PERSPECTIVE

In my mundane obscurity,

Almighty God enters daily my ambiguity,

Permeates the moment ordinary,

Metamorphing its banality.

Expanded vision, enriched heart,

Overwhelming beauty You do impart.

Trees speak, birds sing;

Bring my voice to offering.

Evening sun adorns Your Presence,

Searing awe in my very essence.

Still my Soul, Breath of Splendor;

Paint the moment in Godly candor.

WOODLAND TREASURES

Underneath canopy of green-leafed tree,
    My heart does come to worship Thee.
Send a sign of Your love,
    Shower me with favor from above.

Oh such treasures You brought to me:
    An iridescent green beetle and cricket bending knee;
Ray of sunshine on my face,
    Only confirmation of Your grace.

Grackle, chipmunk chords did blend;
    All the pleasures of earth to you I send.
Boxwood turtle basking in the sun,
    White tail deer on the run.

Turkey gobbles, turning flight;
    Seemingly ordinary things resound Your might.
Be still, sweet girl, take simple pleasure.
    All the earth My love to you cannot measure.

FALL SONG

Color the woods with Your Glory.
    Cloud the skies with Your Story.
        Sing
            Wind
                As
                    Cello
                        Strings
To all of earth Your Joy You bring!

Swaying trees clap and shout
    Hallelujah, Creator's all about.
        Light of Son, warm my soul,
            Illumine truth, annihilate deception's toll.

Speak unique whisperings to my ear.
    Spirit, chase my heart, still me, to hear
        The prompting of gifts to bring forth,
            Lauding my Maker with collaborative rapport.

AUTUMN EPIPHANY

Grey Autumn morn, lane lined with blue-berried Yews, flanked
   with variegated rust and golden Oaks,
Red-dressed Sassafras, Yellow-cloaked Sycamore, fruit-bearing
   Walnuts, clamoring in anticipation.
Street decked in awesome splendor, stopped me dead,
   to tear up and choke.
Trees swaying, applauding, shouting "Holy Emancipation."

Confetti me with shower of leaves,
   as if a private ticker-tape parade.
Singing, praise you, adore you, you are God's valued one,
Lovely girl, come forth; no longer need for masquerade.
I honor you, I cherish you, I lift you through My Son.

Taken aback in delight, my heart gleefully cried:
   "for me Lord, You did this for me?"
Stunned by Your generous gift of worth
   revealed through customized presentation,
My heart can only gulp and resoundingly say,
   "I receive Your Liberty."
You have Joyed my soul beyond wildest expectation.

Magnify You, my voice returns Your Song, glory, glory, glory.
I dance Your Joy, paint Your Love, taste and see Your Goodness.
Live my life so all may see Your Story.
Drink Your Wine, restoring me to wholeness.

GRATITUDE TRANSFORMS VISION

I was barked out of bed in the middle of the night. Grumbling, begrudging this freezing, cold, early morning trek, it seemed challenging to do anything but succumb to major pessimism.

All of this exasperation for a false alarm.

There was no chance of going back to bed another hour before needing to get kids ready for school. My mind was already reeling, planning the day's activities.

Trying to take a quick shower proved to be a mistake, only to be summoned out once again by a needy dog.

On the walk, shivering, frustrated and complaining about losing my life, thinking, "What have I gotten myself into, yada, yada, yada," it occurred to me (probably a divine prodding), to ask God to walk with me and show me the morning.

With this change of attitude, the icy surroundings took on a whole new demeanor. The naked trees against the sky now produced lovely dark silhouettes. Numerous birdcalls and their echoing responses quickened the air with life. White tail and squirrels rustled the leaves of the forest floor. Even the frost on the ground became delightful, and the nipping chill of the wind started to caress my cheeks, my soul, with the pleasure of God's companionship, instead of biting me with cold.

The atmosphere was electric with his presence. What love, that he would join my grumbling heart and transform my frustration.

Later that day, Coco and I were back out pounding the pavement together – he learning to heel, and me ironically also being schooled in the same lesson. To heel: to follow at the heels; chase closely (of a dog); close behind one; under control or subjugation; to cause to learn; to attend, obey.

(more...)

I found it interesting that several people had recommended a particular muzzle leash that forces the dog to heel because of its discomfort – or a choke collar. Our trainer had said, "Well, those methods demand control, but don't really allow the dog to *choose* to obey of his own volition."

Lord, you wouldn't even have joined me on my walk this morning if I hadn't invited you, let alone insisted that I follow at your heels per your command. You want me to choose it.

A delightful poem was born from the gift of beauty and your ubiquitous presence of love and peace on the morning jaunt as you instructed me in the discipline of heeling. Your subtle voice whispered, "I am showing you that this is how to remain in proximity of me all the day long."

Many times, when there has been a sensation or "glimmer" of your nearness, I've thought, "How do I stay, linger and abide there and not quickly retreat?" Fleeting – the experience, connection, the coming together is so pleasurable, intensely rich, one does not want to leave or come down from its euphoric high.

I've long been in the process of learning to be my most authentic self, the one of your composition. The last few days have brought to light the awareness that creating word pictures is your gift, your pleasure, your unique identity for me, and it pleases my soul most intensely. How awesome is that, that you would intend me do something that is totally thrilling, energizing, pleasing, magnificent, wonderful, overwhelmingly grand!

It dawned on me while walking that "being," traversing to the inner-most truth of my created soul, claiming myself – loving my soul, developing and being myself – will keep me in your habitation all the day long; for to "be" I must heel closely, chase and stay beside you, ever cognizant of your every move, complying and knowing that my best interest is your priority, that you protect me, flourish and take care of me, love and desire my presence by your side forever.

The gradations of hues in the sky were magnificent, sending me rummaging through the files in my brain to retrieve the color name that would best describe them – paint them with words. What characterizations would capture that scenario: celestial presence, miraculous transformation, epiphany, divine encounter, spiritual revelation, to change one's thinking, to open one's eyes?

Artistic word pairings presented themselves to me speaking of the beauty and treasures revealed, anchoring them in my mind, allowing procurement when I got home to write them down.

Later, in and amongst the day's errands, reliving these descriptive couplets of the morning's adventure, activated the initial lines of poetry. What delight to delineate the escapade! This made it possible to re-experience that magical walk once again and be awed by the wonder of it.

A lovely poem evolved ...

Ode To A February Morning

Intricate bare branches against winter morning sky,
Bounding white-tail deer on woodland floor, rustling leaves reply.

Frost-laden blades of grass scattered with sugared leaves
Silently sparkle, dazzle, my treasure quest appease.

Scurrying squirrels scamper through forest;
Flocking birds resounding melodic chorus;

Cardinal chirps; chip, chip, mon cherie;
Neighboring friend recants, twilling joyful ecstasy.

Gradations of blue-gray hues backdrop filtered cornstalk light,
Announcing daylight coming forth, oh, glorious sight.

All this and more would I miss,
Had not You I sought. You brought me Bliss!

(continued...)

    Always catching me off guard, who would suspect that you would humor me, preordainly planning for our intricate family needs, by enlisting a dog to enlighten the way for my precious daughter and me? The pure love with which you, God, enter our daily lives customizing the approach, accommodating our divinely orchestrated uniqueness, is mind-boggling.

    Teacher, lover, you've illumined that, in this seeming calamity, gratitude transforms vision or perspective. Not altering the situation, but unveiling my eyes. What a substantial truth to carry through life.

    At the crack of dawn, Coco and I were back outside; I thought, "All right God, I'll be walking past all the same scenery from yesterday. How can I see something new?" Upon entering the brisk air, it was very apparent why you woke me this morning; you had dressed the old path in a new, utterly spectacular, magical, winter garment – and couldn't wait for me to see it. Around every corner lay a splendid surprise of your making. What an adventure. Merci beaucoup!

Winter Twilight

Freshly fallen damp snow blankets ground;
Magically flocked woodlands soften every sound;

Thickly frosted branches, iced in silvery white,
Bedecked for a gala event, this snowy winter nite.

Dusty, powdered, midnight blue, shrouds the evening sky,
Creating alluring aura, enticing one to fly.

Enter in Ethereal-Land, gossamer labyrinth forest;
Dazzling, crystal paradise surrounds in celestial chorus.

CRYSTAL MORNING

Sleet storm raging, woodland coated;
      Dipped, translucent, crystal paraffin.
Swaying timbers creak, ice toted,
      Glistening branches sporting crumpled cellophane.

Glint of morning sun, shimmering thaw commences;
      Primal rivulets of pure water flow.
Forest live, crackling, trickling, incandesces;
      Sugared footprints, intrigue, untold stories sow.

Flash of color: redhead Woody, in undulating rhythm,
      Drops a most magnificent gift in striking feathered pattern.
Rust-tailed hawk navigates tangled boughs in precision,
      Screaming, soaring, proudly gliding, maneuvering turns.

Magical winter-land dazzles my eye.
      Adorned in glass icicles leaned against the sky.
Catch a fleeting glimmer, hold it in your mind;
      Take out at a later date, review events sublime.

Ticker Tape Parade

It was a gloomy, rainy morning; one of those days you just wanted to snuggle under the covers with a good book and a cup of coffee, read for hours; get up, light a fire in the fireplace, cozy-in on the couch and read some more.

A recent realization for me that "music is the key" had been churning over and over in my mind for weeks. Attempting to make sense of this deeply buried, fragmented memory, I ravenously devoured anything musically related.

In the process, I discovered "Piano Guys," and they were loudly playing in the car when I returned home from dropping my daughter off at school early this gray a.m. The music enveloped me, plunging my senses into an intensely electrifying pleasure. It vibrated my soul strings with a gusto previously unknown. I found my fingers air dancing, playing the piano; I was singing the notes at the top of my lungs, ecstatic, filled to the point of overflowing.

Rounding the corner to our house, the exquisite color-decked trees intimately closing in on either side of the lane, coffered overhead with a misty, silvery, clouded ceiling, applauded my arrival – literally coming to life, shouting, and swaying and singing: "You are my beloved one, adored, oh so very cherished."

The swirling leaves and accolades felt like a private ticker-tape parade. This unexpected encounter with a heavenly manifestation – more concisely, Almighty God – brought tears to my eyes and an acutely heightened sense of adoration and praise.

Dumbfounded by his miraculous loving presence, I breathlessly raced into the house to jot down thoughts and words, endeavoring to capture what had just occurred, desperately trying to hold onto my brush with God my Father, so I wouldn't lose the experience:

(more...)

... shower, falling leaves,

applauding, glory, glory, glory,

swaying, singing, shouting,

canopy, cozy, clamoring

      anticipation, blue berried yews,

      pine fragrance, woodland glory,

time stands still, splendor of

the leaves, awe, venerate, exalt,

magnify ...

(continued...)

Could this noteworthy event be summarized in a succinct poem, to hold the moment in time like a marker or a monument, to capture and keep it in my repertoire?

What would be a befitting title for the encounter? The word "epiphany" came to mind: an appearance or manifestation, especially of a deity; a sudden intuitive perception or insight into the reality or essential meaning of something, usually initiated by some simple, homely, or commonplace occurrence such as the autumn trees.

Indeed, the swaying trees and falling leaves sang of God's love and gave proclamation of my value to him. His presence was all around caressing and cherishing me with his adoring embrace! My wish was to stay in the moment, to linger there and deeply drink it in, savoring every last drop.

"Autumn Epiphany" was born out the desire to take possession of this ordained moment in time and eternally package it to be placed in my treasure box, enabling me to fondle, hold, and revisit it. From this point forward, every autumn tree and falling leaf will speak of my value and worth. My God, you know how to please me so much.

Early the next morning, after delivering kids to school, surrounded by soul-warming cello music, senses alerted after yesterday's experience; once again, I was literally ambushed by love, pulling in the gate to our road. Wow! I didn't expect that – tearfully traveling slowly up the road to take in the trees anew. As I hit the blue berried yews, all the words of a poem sprang into my mind once more:

... flanked by variegated rust and golden oaks,
sassafras dressed in red, sycamore cloaked in yellow,
fruit-bearing walnuts,
clamoring in anticipation ...

And the whole ticker-tape parade repeated itself to a full crescendo; tears streaming down my face, being applauded, adored, loved – all the way down the road afresh.

With all my heart and soul I echo the praise back to You;
while cradling myself in my arms, rocking, I say,
Embrace me 3 all of Trinity.

Even in writing this, it is apparent that the shape of the three is an abstract heart!

I wanted to turn around and drive up and down the street for multiple encores.

It's been said that one should not to get too caught up in their work, not to continually re-read it, but a revisiting of these poems is essential to me, because they describe intimate encounters with God. And each time I do, there is a reconnection and reliving of our rendezvous!

Standing back in amazement even in writing these last sentences, the realization that the gift isn't just one moment or a glimmer cast in time but a revolving wardrobe door like C.S. Lewis' "The Lion, the Witch, and the Wardrobe" scenario – where anytime I peruse the words or see an autumn tree, a portal of reentry into the tryst is possible; the words are living!

In the beginning the Word was with God and the Word was God.

EPILOGUE

Travesty Impersonates Truth ... Truth Prevails

Frenzy prances;
    lambasted by unforeseen
        cobwebs of
            insidious entanglement.

Reeling from
    cunning, subtle
        ploy,
raping my spirit
      for another's greedy indigence.

Prisoner from birth.
    Bullied, exploited,
        ensnared, coerced to do the
    captor's needy bidding.

Stripped of my innate essence,
    compromised, tyrannized,
my psychological infrastructure
    perpetrated, infiltrated,
        programmed to comply to
          every beck and call.

Passed from one despotic
    generation to the next;
        no death or separation
      to release from divisive emotional entrapment.

Ragged, torn, weary,
    oh, so very weary,
I must keep walking, keep walking, keep walking, ...

Light of truth
        dance for me,
                draw me out of darkness.
Woo me with Your Music sweet,
        coax me to Your wholeness.

Rewind the bludgeoning of deceit,
        unshackle evil's bondage;
                Sing to my deaf, crippled ear,
                      magnify my vision.

Color beauty all around.
          Profoundly claim Your Glory.
                  Orchestrate Your wondrous Love,
                      heal my wounded story.

Singer chant your melodious song,
        entice my soul to healing;
                come to set the prisoner free,
                    bring my heart to being.

So I will begin singing, singing, singing!

                                                Amen

Truths Along The Path

Through my journey, some of the truths that became clear and dear to me are these:

You prepare a feast for me in the presence of my enemies ...
> My cup overflows with blessings. (Ps. 23:5)

I have been with you wherever you have gone ...
> I will make your name famous ... (I Ch. 17:8)

For the Lord will take delight in you ... his love will calm your fears.
> He will rejoice over you with joyful songs. (Zeph. 3:17)

I will give you treasures hidden in the darkness – secret riches ...
> so you may know that I am the Lord,
> the one who calls you by name. (Is. 45:3)

He will cover you with his feathers ... shelter you with his wings.
> His faithful promises are your armor and protection. (Ps. 91:4)

Do not be afraid of the terrors of the night ... (Ps. 91:5)

The Lord is my refuge, my place of safety; he is my God,
> and I trust him. (Ps. 91:2)

The light shines in the darkness,
> and the darkness can never extinguish it. (Jn. 1:5)

I am leaving with you a gift – peace of mind and heart. (Jn. 14:27)

He lifted me out of the pit of despair, out of the mud and the mire.
> He set my feet on solid ground and steadied me
> as I walked along. He has given me a new song to sing ...
> Many will see what he has done and be amazed. (Ps. 40:2-3)

You have turned my mourning into joyful dancing ... (Ps. 30:11)

He heals all my diseases. (Ps. 103:3)

I will give you back your health and heal your wounds ... (Jer. 30:17)

He will show you which path to take. (Prov. 3:5-6)

I will be found by you, says the Lord. (Jer. 29:13)

The Lord your God will ... neither fail nor abandon you. (Deut. 31:6)

Taste and see that the Lord is good ... (Ps. 34:8)

I will be your friend ... counselor ... guide ... shepherd ...
> lover of your soul ... advocate ... groom ...
> (Jn. 15:15; Isa. 9:16; Ps. 119:105; Ps. 23:1;
> Jn. 3:16; Jn 15:26; Rev. 19:7)

Even if my father and mother abandon me,
> the Lord will hold me close. (Ps. 27:10)

IN GRATITUDE

To my dear husband, **Steve**, who has always believed in and encouraged me. Merci beaucoup! Rather than balking at the horrific events of my life, you have unflinchingly stood by my side, consoling, applauding, and enabling me to continue the battle of replacing lies with truth, fortifying me with love and prayer. So very blessed am I to have a husband of such remarkable character – as the captain of our ship, and soul mate of my heart. You are my special angel from God!

To my children, **Taylor** and **Monique**, you are such a special gift in my life. You continually inspire me and stimulate my personal growth. Thank you for your patience with this project and your belief that I could do it.

To my treasured friend, **Sarah Rowan**, who consistently celebrates the good and the bad in life equally. You have spoken volumes to me in my quest for healing and becoming. You lovingly attended dear Joseph, your Alzheimer's husband, for ten-plus years, transitioning this personal life crisis into a significant worldwide cause through The Eden Alternative. Thank you, dear Sarah, for your love, courage, and example. I deeply cherish and admire you.

To my courageous sister, **Marilyn Dekam**, who survived the same harrowing life as mine, you have exhibited the greatest bravery in entering the process of overcoming and conquering. And, through it all, you have never lost your sense of wonder and awe of the beauty around you.

To **Dr. Ron** and **Linda Sprunger**, who were an absolute delight, generously giving of their amazing musical talents. I am indebted to you both for writing the arrangement for *"Draw Me Out of Darkness."*

To **Beth Cantrell**, you are wonderfully unique in that you walk along side me sharing my daily life, whether it be running errands, cooking dinner, or analyzing my writings. Thanks for lavishly offering your time, love, sage advice, listening skills, and intellectual and spiritual stimulation.

To **Ellen Craig**, **Liz McEwen**, **Bette DeHaven**, **Ruth Milliron**, **Brenda Holler**, **Lori Brown**, **Linda Kane**, **Michele** and **Marissa Mac**, **Donna Gates**, and **Joyce Clouse** – some of the most exceptional women I know. Each in your own way has brought great enrichment and support to my life and this project.

To graphic art student, **Olivia Duvall**, for assisting me early in the process of beginning to bring my ideas to fruition. Your talent, patience and generosity are deeply appreciated.

To **Kimberly Noah**, graphic designer and production artist for this book, thank you for adding your exquisite attention to detail, and your personal concern for its polish and finessing.

To **Marti Healy**, talented author and editor, I am indebted to you for your ability to capture the essence of my story of emergence, reframing and organizing it with a clarity that will enable it to take flight in the hearts and minds of its readers. All the while, you have honored and maintained the integrity of my voice. What an amazing gift. An added bonus is the friendship that has developed during this process.

To **Barry Doss**, my publisher at The Design Group Press, my gratitude for your generosity and personal attention while masterfully overseeing the conceptualization, design, layout and production of this book, bringing it to its ultimate completion. Your belief in me, and your prompting to produce at a higher level, has grown me personally and in my craft, and has drawn out creativity in me that has been long buried. You have challenged me to dig deep, continually striving for more. I am awed by the professional talents and capability with which you have executed this project.

With undying appreciation and forever love to you all,

Cindy